FRED FLINTSTONE'S ADVENTURES with PULLEYS

Work Smarter, Not Harder

by Mark Weakland

illustrated by Paco Sordo

CAPSTONE PRESS
a capstone imprint

Good Morning, Bedrock!
Today I could use any number of simple machines—a wedge, an inclined plane, a wheel and axle, a screw, or a lever. But something tells me today is going to be a great day for using pulleys.

Pulleys on this exercise machine change the direction of force.

Morning, Fred!

Morning, Barney! Just look at how that turning pulley wheel allows me to do work. Isn't it great? As the wheel in the pulley rotates, the cord moves in either direction. A pulley lets me move things up and down, like this flag.

A pulley on a flagpole lets you raise and lower the flag.

Yabba-dabba-doo! When one pulley isn't enough, I use two. Using multiple pulleys makes work easier. The pulleys lessen the force needed to lift heavy things. If I use two pulleys, I can use half as much force to lift this heavy sail.

Like other simple machines, pulleys decrease the amount of force I need to use. The effort I use to pull is called the input force. The pulleys produce an output force. This force lifts the load: the sail!

A block and tackle uses pulleys to lift all types of heavy objects.

Hold on, Barney! You're working too hard. Step aside and let me show you how it's done.

Aye, aye Fred.

Sometimes a block and tackle is best. It decreases the amount of force needed to lift a heavy object. The weight of the object is split equally between the two pulleys. I only have to use half as much force to lift the boat. Now that's the Fred Flintstone way!

BOAT MARINA

Pulleys and ropes allow rock climbers to defy gravity.

Glossary

defy—to resist

effort—the force applied to a machine to do work

force—a push or pull exerted upon an object

gravity—a force that pulls objects together

inclined plane—a slanting surface that is used to move objects to different levels

input force—the initial force used to get a machine working

load—an object that moves when a force is applied

multiple—involving many parts or many things

output force—also called the load; the weight of the object to be moved

pulley—a grooved wheel turned by a rope, belt, or chain that often moves heavy objects

rappel—to slide down a strong rope

reduce—to make something smaller or less in amount or size

rotate—to spin around

Read More

LaMachia, Dawn. *Pulleys at Work.* Zoom in on Simple Machines. New York: Enslow Publishing, 2016.

Oxlade, Chris. *Making Machines with Pulleys.* Simple Machine Projects. Chicago: Capstone Raintree, 2015.

Weakland, Mark. *Smash!: Wile E. Coyote Experiments with Simple Machines.* Wile E. Coyote, Physical Science Genius. North Mankato, Minn.: Capstone Press, 2014.

Internet Sites

FactHound offers a safe, fun way to find Internet sites related to this book. All of the sites on FactHound have been researched by our staff.

Here's all you do:

Visit *www.facthound.com*

Type in this code: 9781491484753

Super-cool stuff! Check out projects, games and lots more at **www.capstonekids.com**

Index

Look for all the books in the series:

Thanks to our adviser for his expertise, research, and advice:
Paul Ohmann, PhD, Associate Professor of Physics
University of St. Thomas, St. Paul, Minnesota

Published in 2016 by Capstone Press, A Capstone Imprint
1710 Roe Crest Drive, North Mankato, Minnesota 56003
www.mycapstone.com

Library of Congress Cataloging-in-Publication Data
Weakland, Mark, author.
  Fred Flintstone's adventures with pulleys : work smarter, not
harder / by Mark Weakland ; illustrated by Paco Sordo.
  pages cm — (Flintstones explain simple machines)
Summary: "Popular cartoon character Fred Flintstone explains
how pulleys work and how he uses simple machines in his
daily life"—Provided by publisher.
Audience: 6–8.
Audience: K to grade 3.
ISBN 978-1-4914-8475-3 (library binding)
ISBN 978-1-4914-8481-4 (eBook PDF)
1. Pulleys—Juvenile literature. 2. Simple machines—
Juvenile literature. I. Sordo, Paco, illustrator. II. Title. III.
Title: Adventures with pulleys. IV. Series: Weakland, Mark.
Flintstones explain simple machines.
TJ1103.W43 2016
621.8—dc23   2015024734

Editorial Credits
Editor: Alesha Halvorson
Designer: Ashlee Suker
Creative Director: Nathan Gassman
Media Researcher: Tracy Cummins
Production Specialist: Kathy McColley

The illustrations in this book were created digitally.

Image Credits
Shutterstock: Anna Omelchenko, 19, Christin Lola, 9, holbox,
7, Volodymyr Kyrylyuk, 16

Printed in the United States of America in
North Mankato, MN. 092015 009221CGS16